TABLE OF CONTENTS

CRUISING GUIDE PUBLICATIONS

The Leeward Islands

The Leeward Islands of the Caribbean include 10 main islands that embrace Anguilla to the north and west, and then gently curving south to Dominica. The islands are rich in their history as well as diverse in their cultures and languages. To visit them, one ideally needs several months. Few of us are blessed with that opportunity.

The variety offers the cruiser a myriad of choices. Anchorages in the Leewards can be near sophisticated, European-style cities, or off of deserted white sand beaches with only the pelicans diving around your boat. Both are accessible within a short sail of each other.

Sailing conditions do vary somewhat. The tradewinds are less lively in the northern islands making for a more leisurely sail. Further south the tradewinds become more vigorous allowing for an exhilarating romp.

Leeward Anchorages is the companion guide to the *Cruising Guide to the Leeward Islands*. Both books are written by Chris Doyle. Chris has been writing guides to the Caribbean for over 25 years. He diligently sails from island to island to research and record all the latest information.

In this book we followed the format of the *Cruising Guide to the Leeward Islands*, so that you may cross-reference the books if you wish. We begin in what we call the Renaissance Islands of Anguilla, St. Martin, Sint Maarten, and St. Barts.

The next group of islands we have dubbed the Islands that Brush the Clouds, including the islands of Saba, Statia (St. Eustatius), St. Kitts (St. Christopher), Nevis and Montserrat (famous for it's active volcano).

Going south, we have called the southern-most islands in the group the Islands of

Traditional dress in Karukera.

Mountains and Mangroves. Starting with Antigua and Barbuda, Guadeloupe and the Saintes, we end with the island of Dominica.

We hope that this book provides you with a viewpoint that gives you a great perspective on the anchorages you will be visiting. It will also give you a taste of the beauty of the Leeward Islands of the Caribbean. These diverse and beautiful islands are waiting for you to discover them.

Welcome to the Caribbean!
Nancy Scott
Publisher

Oualie Beach anchorage.

Saba's houses cling to the steep mountainsides.

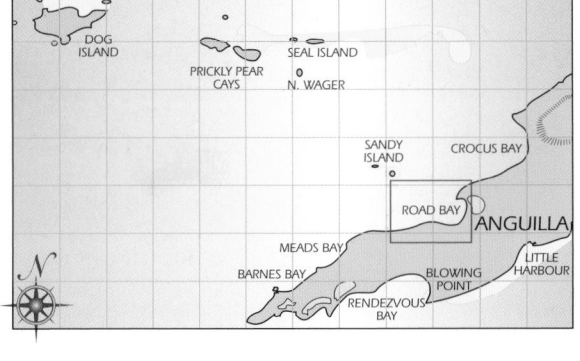

Road Bay is a charming, peaceful anchorage fringed by a perfect powdery beach. Along the beach you will find Sandy Ground Village, a fine collection of bars and restaurants plus a few shops. Behind the beach are salt ponds that support a wonderful array of egrets and wading birds. This is the main port of entry for yachts and one of the most pleasant anchorages in the northern Leeward Islands.

As you approach Road Bay keep clear of the shoals along the southern shore. Otherwise the bay is wide open. Avoid the northern tip of the bay, which is shoal. You can anchor anywhere in the bay except in the main shipping passage. Road Bay is normally an excellent overnight anchorage. Keep in mind that there can be loud music from the bars ashore until 0130 from Wednesday to Sunday. The light on the northern headland occasionally goes out late at night when the batteries are beyond their prime.

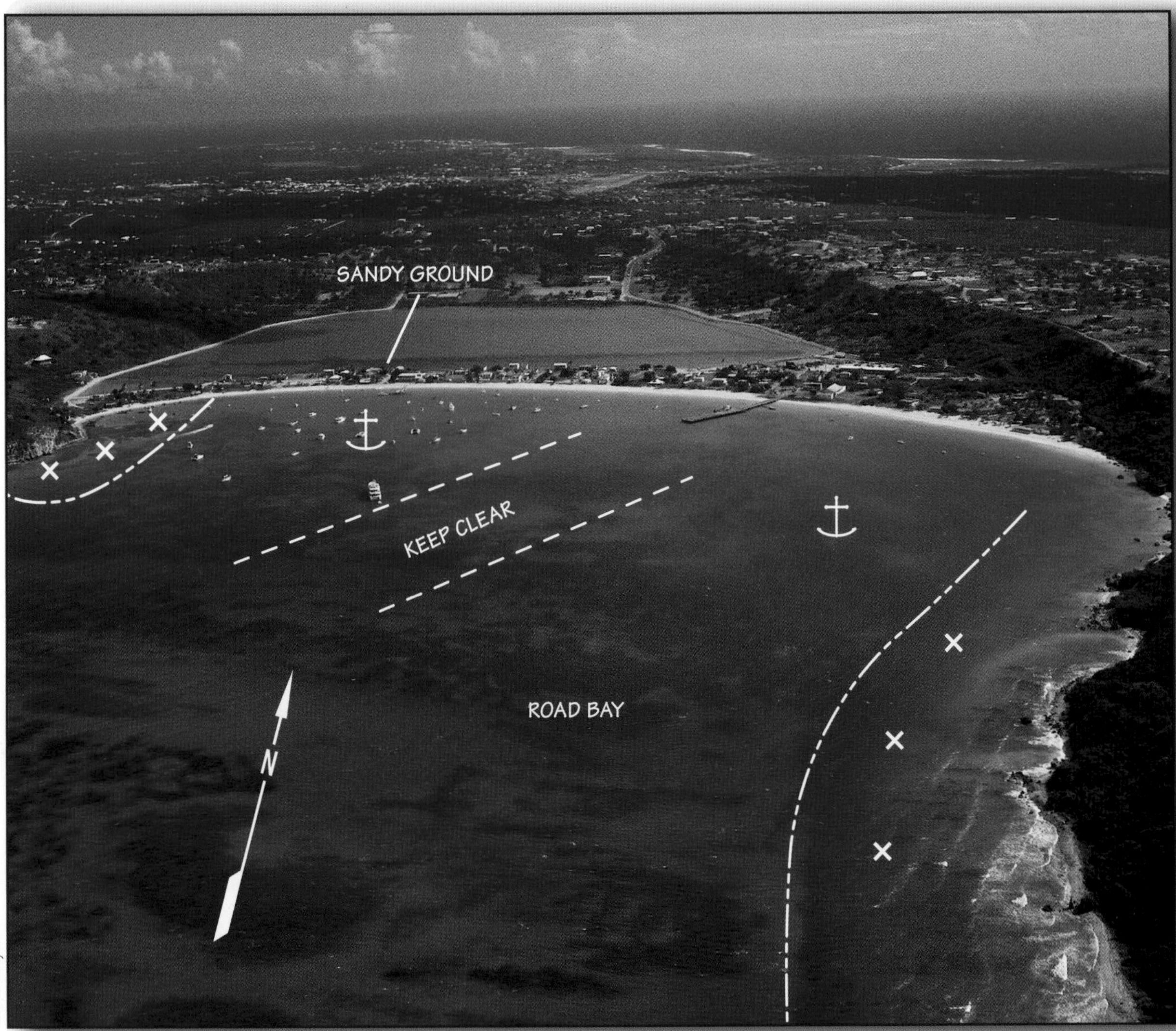

Chris Doyle

Sandy Island, Anguilla

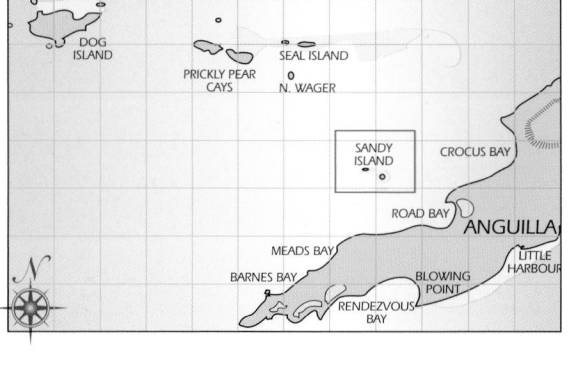

Sandy Island, a circle of sand with a few baby palm trees, lies about a mile to the north of Anguilla, just before Road Bay. There are both shoals and reefs here, so only approach in good light conditions.

A coral island, about five feet high, is clearly visible to the northwest of Sandy Island. The water around this island has many coral heads, especially in the southeasterly direction. Give it wide clearance. A 5-foot shoal lies to the south of Sandy Island, which is clearly visible as turquoise water. Do not cross this, even in a shoal draft boat, as it generates large waves, which sometimes break. Sandy Island is surrounded by reef, which is quite visible. Do not approach too closely.

Anchoring around Sandy Island is regulated because of possible damage to underwater reefs. The only permissible anchoring area suitable for yachts is indicated on the photograph. Mooring buoys are provided, but if there are not enough buoys, you can anchor in the same area. Make sure you are anchored on an area of clear sand with no coral heads.

Chris Doyle

Cornelius Schoonbeek

To the east of Road Bay there is an attractive sweeping bay some two miles long. Crocus Bay is the most protected part of this and an excellent overnight anchorage. Ashore is Ray's Place, a good, reasonably priced restaurant, and an excellent beach and snorkeling.

If you are approaching along the coast from Road Bay, stay a few hundred yards offshore till you pass Katouche Bay, as shoals extend 60 yards or more offshore. If you are approaching from out to sea, Crocus Bay has a paved road which runs up the hill. A big square apartment block sits on top of the hill and at the left hand end of the beach is a large tin building which houses a water desalinization plant. Anchor anywhere off Crocus Bay Beach south of Pelican Point. Anchor a fair way out as the wind can drop and a swell could carry your yacht toward the shore. Use plenty of scope. You can beach your dinghy just outside Roy's Place. The beach is calm except for occasional winter swells.

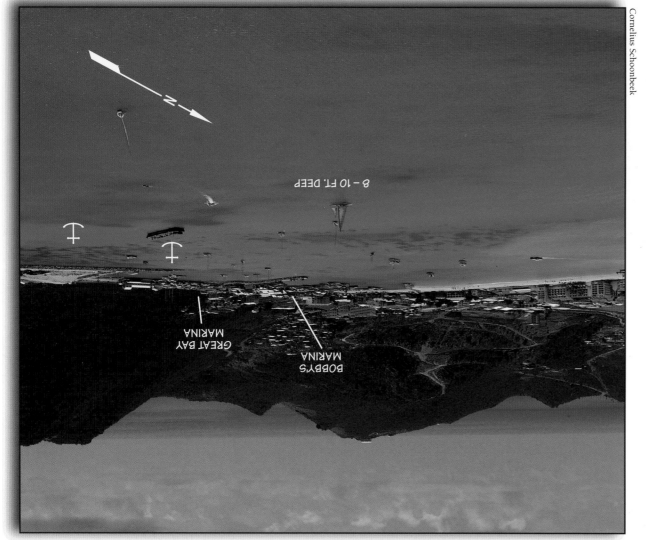

Cornelius Schoonbeek

8 - 10 FT. DEEP

GREAT BAY
MARINA

BOBBY'S
MARINA

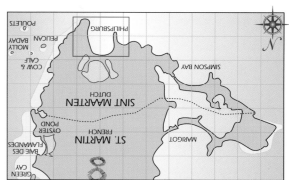

Philipsburg is the capital of St. Maarten and lies at the head of Great Bay. It is both a major cruise ship stop and a popular stop for yachts. The yachting center is in the northeastern corner in the general area of Great Bay Marina and Bobby's Marina. Waterfront bars abound. There are plans to turn these two marinas into one giant marina suitable for mega-yachts.

The best way to approach is to pass close by the new cruise shop dock and then head towards Great Bay Marina. Depths reduce suddenly from 30 feet to about 10 feet, then become rather bumpy, mainly between 8 and 10 feet, all the way in. Both marinas have done some dredging and are deeper than the approaches: Bobby's is now mainly 15 feet deep and Great Bay Marina has about 17 feet at the deepest part, shoaling to about 7 feet in the southern corner. Philipsburg is a good anchorage in most conditions. However, it gets very rolly when the wind switches to southeast. Philipsburg is not the place to be during dangerous weather conditions.

Simpson Bay, Sint Maarten

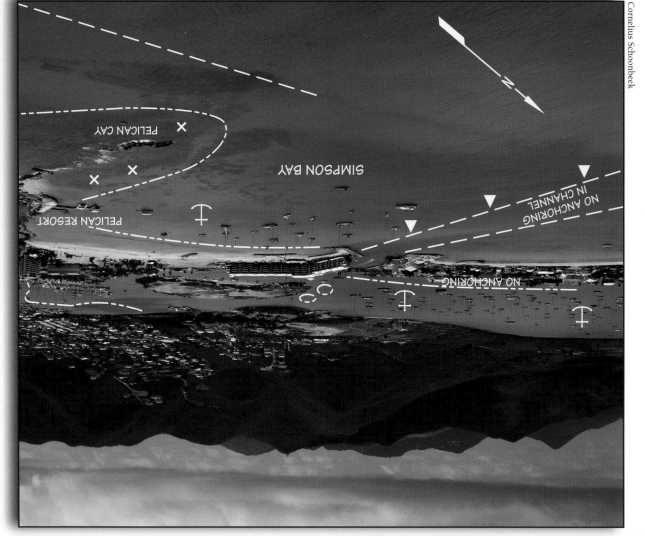

Cornelius Schoonbeek

PELICAN CAY

SIMPSON BAY

PELICAN RESORT

NO ANCHORING
IN CHANNEL

NO ANCHORING

N

GREEN CAY

BAIE DES FLAMMANDES

OYSTER POND

ST. MARTIN FRENCH

MARIGOT

COW & CALF

MOLLY BADAY

PELICAN

SINT MAARTEN DUTCH

SIMPSON BAY

PHILIPSBURG

POULETS

N

Simpson Bay is a large and pleasant bay surrounded by beaches. The eastern part makes a good sheltered anchorage. Simpson Bay Lagoon offers about 12 square miles of completely protected land locked water. Access is by a canal and swing bridge from Simpson Bay. The entrance channel has been dredged to 16 feet. Simpson Bay Lagoon is the yachting center of St. Maarten. Most Dutch side marinas and marine businesses surround the Lagoon on the Dutch side. You can dinghy or take your boat to Marigot, which is the French side center of yachting.

When approaching Simpson Bay from the east, swing out in an arc well outside Pelican Point and Pelican Cay. When you are past the island, head into the anchorage between Pelican Resort and the bridge. Don't head up too sharply as there is a wreck of a barge with 7.5 feet of water over it just north of Pelican Cay. Holding in the anchorage is good in sand, nine to 14 feet deep. This is a good overnight anchorage that is not too bad even in southeasterly winds.

Marigot, Saint Martin

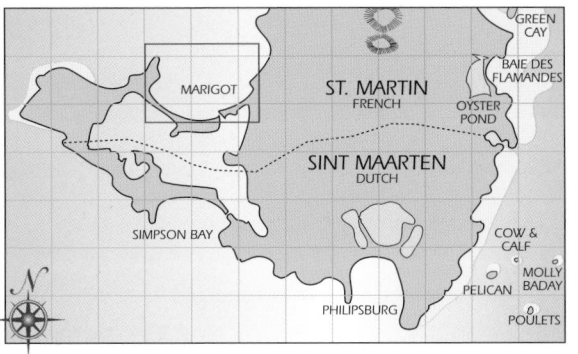

Marigot is the capital of the French side of St. Martin. It has the feeling of a fashionable Riviera seaport town. The bustling town is full of duty free shops, boutiques, restaurants and an attractive waterfront market. Although there are always many boats in the anchorage, there is always plenty of room.

The approach is wide open and free from dangers during the day. At night there are several unlit steel buoys to avoid. Two of these are mooring buoys for ships. The outer one is at 18 ° 04.88'N, 63 ° 06.31' W. The other is a little further south. On the other side of the bay there is an unlit IALA buoys marking a 15 foot shoal at 18° 05.26', 63° 05.67'W.

The water starts shelving a long way offshore, but you can carry eight or nine feet right in close to town. The wind can change here so leave plenty of swinging room. Leave a clear passage for the ferries and the marina entrance. During the winter months a swell can occasionally make it uncomfortable.

There is access to Simpson Bay Lagoon via an opening bridge just west of the little cliff to the west of the town. The bridge opens Monday to Saturday at 0900, 1400 and 1730; on Sundays and holidays, and from November to the end of June at 0900 and 1730.

Cornelius Schoonbeek

MARIGOT

PORT LA ROYALE

FORT LOUIS

FERRY TERMINAL

Marina under construction.

BAIE DU MARIGOT

N

Grande Case, Saint Martin

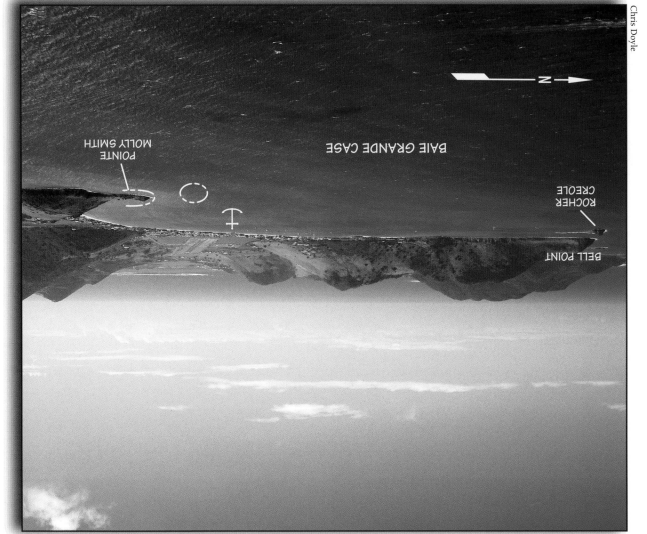

Chris Doyle

POINTE
MOLLY SMITH

BAIE GRANDE CASE

ROCHER
CREOLE

BELL POINT

N

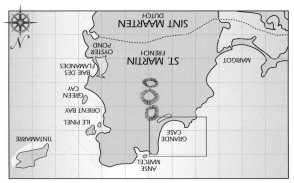

TINTAMARRE

ANSE
MARCEL

N

ILE PINEL

BAIE DES
FLAMANDES

GREEN
CAY

ORIENT BAY

OYSTER
POND

ST. MARTIN
FRENCH

SINT MAARTEN
DUTCH

GRANDE
CASE

MARIGOT

Baie Grand Case is a long sweeping beach-fronted bay and the town is known as the gastronomic center of St. Martin, so be prepared to eat out. The anchorage is generally good for overnighting, though it can be rolly. Grand Case is home of the small French airport.

The northern end of the bay gets some protection from Rocher Creole, a conspicuous rock-island some 100 feet high. There are underwater rocks close to the island. It is best to pass outside Rocher Creole though you can find a passage some 8 feet deep between the island and Bell Point.

From the south, keep at least half a mile off the headland (Pointe Molly Smith) as there is a shoal several hundred yards to its northwest.

Anchor anywhere off the town docks in sand and weed. Ashore you will find the street is packed with some wonderful restaurants from elegant and expensive to cute and inexpensive.

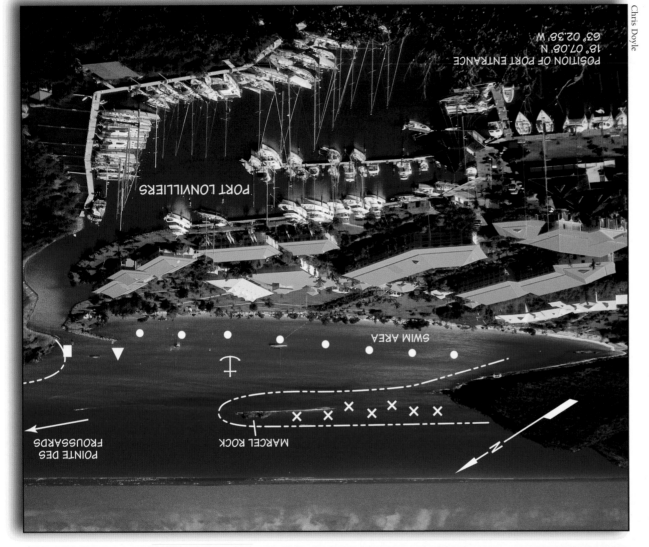

POSITION OF PORT ENTRANCE
18° 07.08' N
63° 02.38' W

Chris Doyle

PORT LONVILLIERS

SWIM AREA

MARCEL ROCK

POINTE DES
FROUSSARDS

N

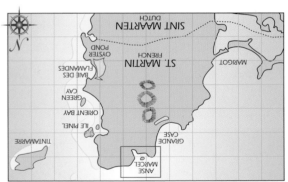

TINTAMARRE

MARGOT

ST. MARTIN
FRENCH

BAIE DES
FLAMANDES

GREEN
CAY

ORIENT BAY

ILE PINEL

GRANDE
CASE

ANSE
MARCEL

OYSTER
POND

SINT MAARTEN
DUTCH

N

Anse Marcel is a small bay with a beach, two hotels and an exclusive marina, Port Lonvilliers. The outer bay anchorage is pretty with a sand beach and turquoise water. If you love jet skis you will find lots of company. The Port Lonvilliers marina is small, well protected, and well maintained.

Exercise caution when approaching from Margot. After passing Bell Point, head way over toward Pointe des Froussards to go around Marcel Rock (about 15 feet high) before turning into the bay. There is a small bay and beach before this rock, which can cause confusion. This rock has also been confused with the 118 foot Rocher Creole off Bell Point. Anse Marcel is reasonably well protected, though a surge does get in, especially in the winter months. Anchoring is tricky as the bottom sand is covered in thick weed. In addition, the wind swings from all directions.

The entrance to Port Lonvilliers marina is by a clearly marked narrow channel. The channel is about quarter of a mile long and ten feet deep. There is only room for one yacht at a time, so sound your horn before entering. There can be some shoaling between dredgings.

Chris Doyle

Tintamarre is a flatish island about 120 feet high and just over a mile long. There is a superb beach along its western shore that you will see very clearly if you are approaching from the west. The southwestern point of Tintamarre has a reef extending from it, which is easily identified by a small sand cay. The reef extends well beyond the sand cay, so give it a wide clearance. A bank of sand and weed suitable for anchoring extends several hundred yards from the beach. Depths start at 24 feet and slowly shelve toward the shore. Normally you can anchor in here for lunch, and overnight in calm conditions, though it can roll. In heavy swells you may want to give it a miss. The calmest spot is off the northern part of the beach. Those who don't like rolling should prepare a picnic in advance and head in when the yacht is secure. Landing the dinghy can be risky in swells. The beach is open to the public, but the island is privately owned. Cruise ships occasionally pull in here sending hundreds of passengers ashore. If you find the crowds too much, go to Orient Bay and return the next day.

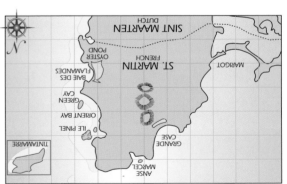

ANSE MARCEL
GRANDE CASE
TINTAMARRE
ILE PINEL
ORIENT BAY
GREEN CAY
BAIE DES FLAMANDES
MARIGOT
ST. MARTIN
FRENCH
OYSTER POND
SINT MAARTEN
DUTCH
N

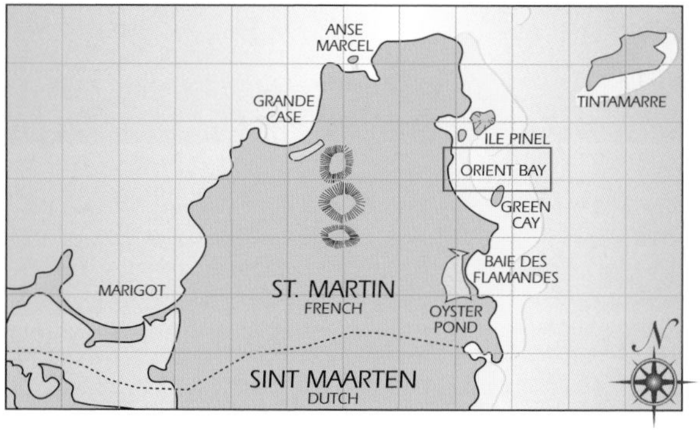

Orient Bay is large, open to the east, with frequent rolling onshore seas. However, there are two protected anchorages: behind Ile Pinel and Green Cay. As the entrance is unprotected, it is unwise to enter this bay when rough. Do not enter with the sun in your eyes. This area is where boats have problems. Six were lost one year, trying to enter south of Green Cay or being rolled in big seas east of Pinel. Take care going into Ile Pinel. Many yachts try to go around the wrong side of Petite Clef and run aground. From the beach at Tintamarre, steer a course of 230° magnetic, to take you in the direction of Green Cay. The entrance channel is on a line between the southern tip of Tintamarre and an aerial on a high ridge south of the highest mountain you can see. The bearing is 255° magnetic to the aerial going in and 75° magnetic south of Tintamarre coming out. Other aerials are lower down, if you have doubts, head for the highest peak instead. Approaching, you will see two developments on your starboard bow. One has green roofs, and the other has white buildings. Getting closer, you will see Green Cay and see the breaking water on the surrounding reef. Sail around the north of this reef and Green Cay.

Chris Doyle

N

PINEL

TINTAMARRE

GREEN CAY

ILE PINEL ANCHORAGE

N

NO PASSAGE

LOCAL BOATS ONLY

SHOAL

SHOAL

Ile Pinel, Saint Martin

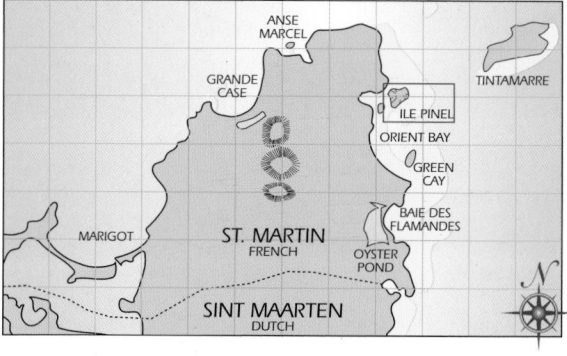

Ile Pinel anchorage is good for an overnight stop, though sometimes rolly. It is a perfect Robinson Crusoe island with sandy beaches, palms and hills, the highest one rising to about 100 feet. Closer to shore, Petite Clef is rocky, and inaccessible. The anchorage is between these islands. It is delightful, but there is barely room for a dozen boats.

Besides the boats in Ile Pinel, you can see many more anchored well to the west of Ile Pinel, behind Petite Clef. This shoal anchorage is reached through a twisty reef-strewn passage to the north of Ile Pinel. It is strictly an anchorage for local boats with intimate knowledge of the reefs. However, the presence of these yachts causes a lot of confusion. Once inside Orient Bay, do not head into Pinel until you are alongside Green Island and can see right up into the lee of Ile Pinel. Make sure you can distinguish boats anchored here from those inside Petite Clef. And make sure you have correctly identified Ile Pinel and Petite Clef. Do not attempt to go inside Petite Clef or Little Pelican from the south, as it is all shoal. There is also a 4-foot shoal right at the entrance to the Ile Pinel anchorage, marked with a small buoy. Pass to port of the shoal and you will arrive ready to anchor.

Cornelius Schoonbeek

⚓ 18° 06.25'N 63° 01.00'W

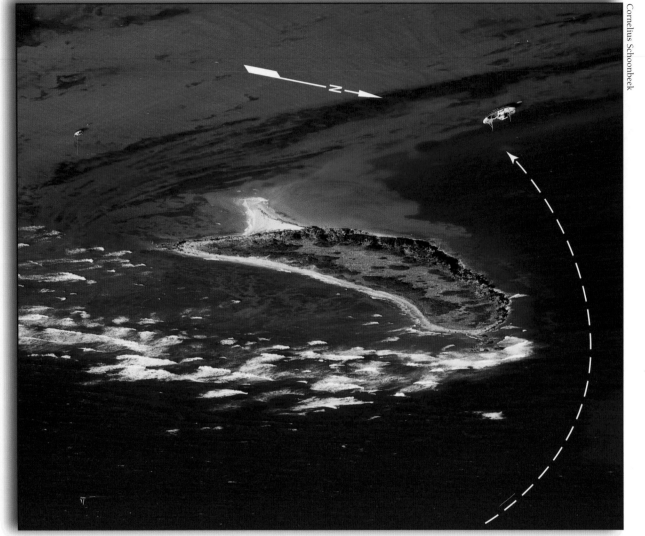

Cornelius Schoonbeek

Green Cay is a low-lying island with a sandy beach at one end. To its south is the long and lovely Orient Beach, the liveliest beach in St. Martin with a colorful holiday atmosphere. The beach is lined with small, cheerfully painted restaurants and bars, shops selling gaily-colored t-shirts, and various water sports facilities.

Approach Green Cay as directed on the Orient Bay page, and make sure you avoid the long reef on its eastern side. Do not turn in till you can see right into the anchorage and Orient beach.

You can anchor in the lee of Green Cay or go on a bit further and drop hook between Green Cay and Orient Beach. It shoals as you go in. This is not a particularly well protected spot, and you would not want to be here in a heavy northerly swell, but on a normal day it makes a good lunch time stop, and you can anchor overnight in settled weather. A series of yellow buoys protect swimmers from jet skis, speedboats and dinghies. Make sure you dinghy in through the marked channel at the eastern end of this area.

(See also: Orient Bay)

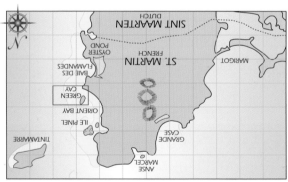

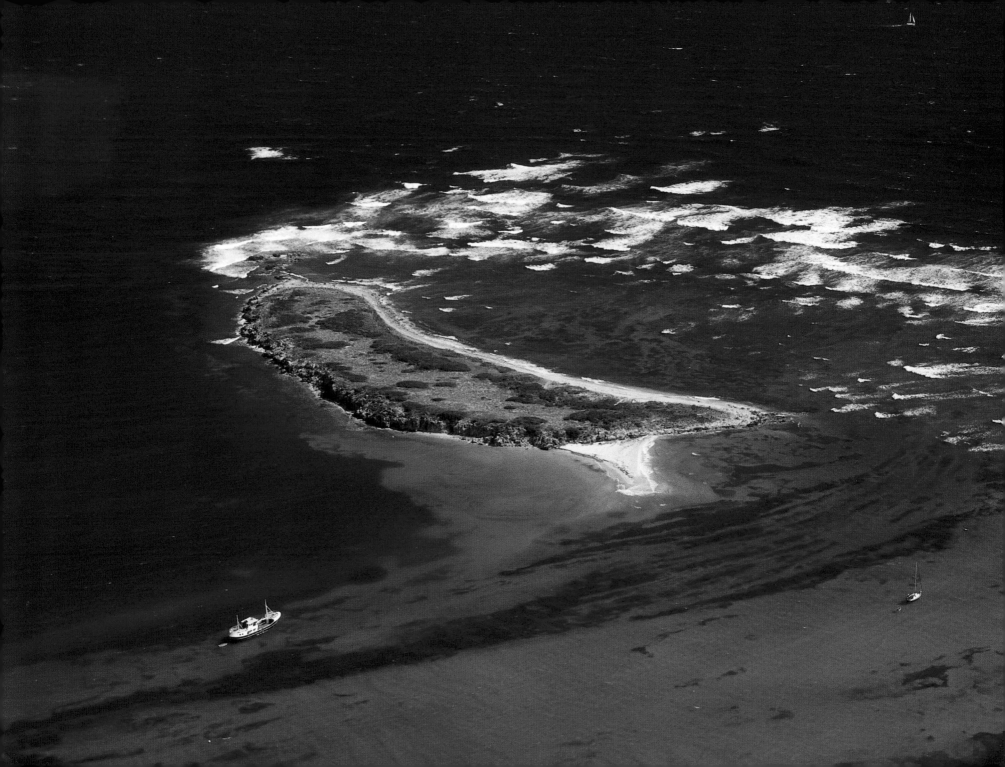

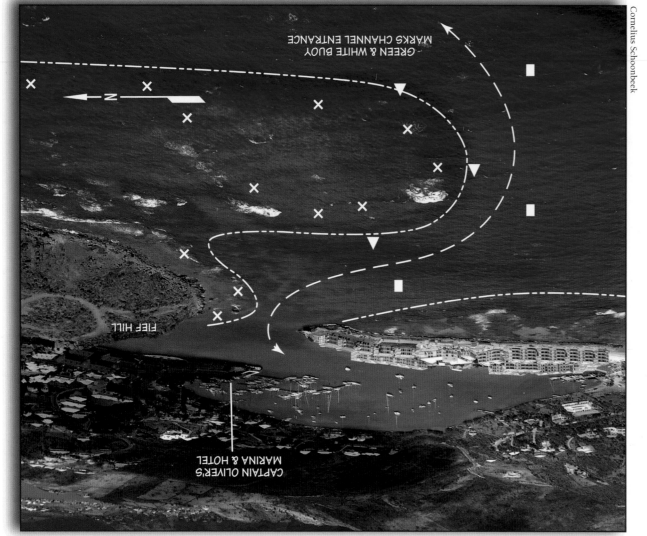

Cornelius Schoonbeek

GREEN & WHITE BUOY
MARKS CHANNEL ENTRANCE

N

FIEF HILL

CAPTAIN OLIVER'S
MARINA & HOTEL

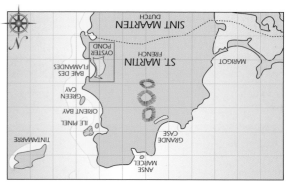

SINT MAARTEN
DUTCH

ST. MARTIN
FRENCH

OYSTER
POND

BAIE DES
FLAMANDES

GREEN
CAY

ORIENT BAY

ILE PINEL

GRANDE
CASE

TINTAMARRE

ANSE
MARCEL

MARIGOT

N

Oyster Pond is a well-protected bay with a marina, restaurants and a market. You really have to be attentive on the approach. Sometimes you have to run down wind through steep seas onto a lee shore dotted with reefs. Occasionally the seas get so bad they break right across the entrance. Even at the best of times, this is no place to make a mistake and you must be absolutely sure you have everything correctly placed before you enter. The entrance is marked by privately maintained markers; an outer green and white buoy, and a channel marked by three red posts and three green posts. Until you see them, don't even think of going in.

From the north keep well outside the reef off Fief Hill until you can identify the markers. Go first to the outer green and white buoy and pass close to it, then proceed between the red and green markers.

From the south you can identify Oyster Pond from the row of many prominent square shaped buildings on the low land (part of a Resort). If you are coming from the south, keep well out in deep water as if you were going to sail right by Oyster Pond. Turn in when you can enter as if from the north.

Ile Fourchue lies conveniently between St. Martin and St. Barts and makes a perfect lunch stop. It is dry and rocky with several steep hills and craggy peaks. There is nothing here except goats who have devoured everything except the rock and the prickles.

The island has a good-sized bay protected from the north and east. The swell can creep in and make it somewhat rolly, though this may usually be lessened with a stern anchor. There is a rock awash off the southern headland and it is best to leave this to starboard when you enter. The anchorage is in the middle of the bay in 20 to 30 feet of water on a sand and weed bottom. Use the yellow Marine Park yacht moorings when available. Ile Fourchue is part of the St. Barts Marine Reserve therefore, spearfishing, jet or water skiing and damaging coral is strictly forbidden. There are also moorings for snorkelers and divers.

Cornelius Schoonbeek

ROCK AWASH

ILE FOURCHUE

N

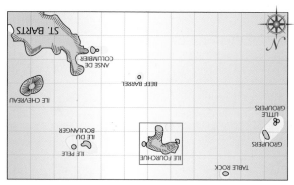

N

TABLE ROCK

GROUPERS

LITTLE GROUPERS

ILE FOURCHUE

ILE PELE

ILE DU BOULANGER

BEEF BARREL

ANSE DE COLUMBIER

ST. BARTS

ILE CHEVREAU

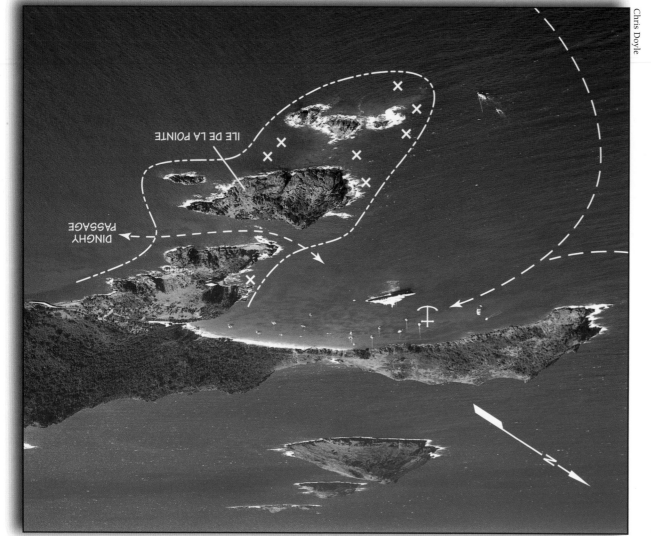

Chris Doyle

ILE DE LA POINTE

DINGHY PASSAGE

This secluded bay has a perfect beach backed by a smattering of palms and a steep hill. There is no road access and the only way to get here, is by boat or a mile- long trek over the hills. Anse de Columbier is part of the St. Barts Marine Reserve. Spearfishing, jet or water skiing and damaging corals are strictly forbidden.

Anse de Columbier is a well-protected anchorage and a good overnight spot. However, during the winter months northerly swells occasionally find their way in and make it somewhat uncomfortable. Ile de la Pointe lies just to the west of the southern headland, and a series of rocks extend beyond the island. Some of these are quite visible, others are awash and some lie just beneath the surface, so pass outside all the visible rocks by a good hundred yards when running between Anse de Colombier and Gustavia.

Use the yellow Marine Park moorings when available. The calmest area is the northeast corner. The wind swings round, especially in the south of the bay, so do not anchor too close to the beach. You can anchor in 15 – 25 feet of water in good holding sand and weed.

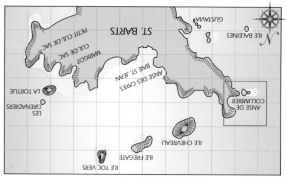

Gustavia, Saint Barts

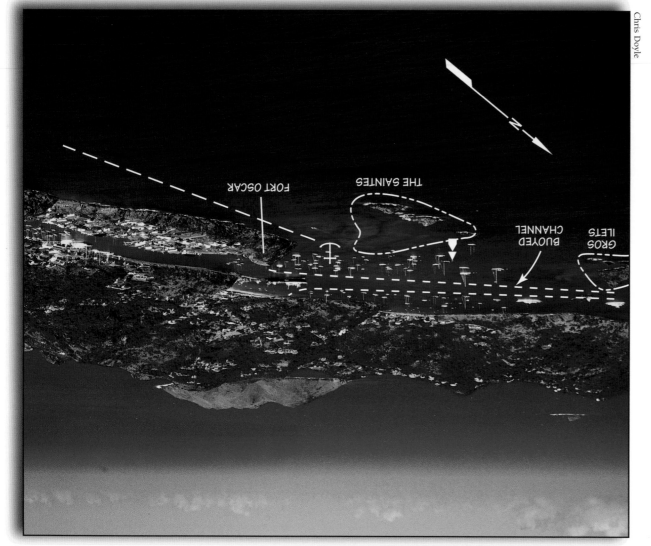

Chris Doyle

FORT OSCAR

THE SAINTES

BUOYED CHANNEL

GROS ILETS

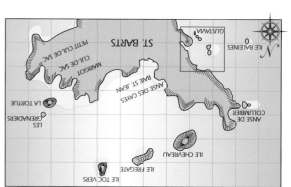

ST. BARTS

GUSTAVIA

ILE BALEINES

PETIT CUL-DE SAC

CUL-DE SAC

MARIGOT

BAIE ST. JEAN

ANSE DES CAYES

LA TORTUE

LES GRENADIERS

ANSE DE COLUMBIER

ILE CHEVREAU

ILE FREGATE

ILE TOC VERS

Gustavia, the main town in St. Barts, is a charming, small French port. It has the reputation of hosting the rich and famous. Many hotels, restaurants and fancy shops are priced to suit them. There are several offshore rocks and islands. If you are approaching from the north, the easiest way is to come inside them. La Baleine is marked by a buoy. To be on the safe side, avoid going between this buoy and Gros Ilets. If you are approaching from the south, there is enough water to pass between the Saintes and the mainland, but shoal water extends well out from the Saintes, so follow along the mainland shore. Do not try to go between the Saintes and the yellow and black buoy which marks a rock to their north. Approaching Gustavia be prepared to thread through anchored boats unless you come in the buoyed channel.

Gustavia is so popular that anchoring can be a problem during the winter. You can anchor off Fort Oscar to its northwest or behind the marked area between Anse Corossol and the fairway to the public dock. Or go stern to one of the long new sections of dock built for visiting yachts on both sides of the harbor. Moorings are sometimes available.

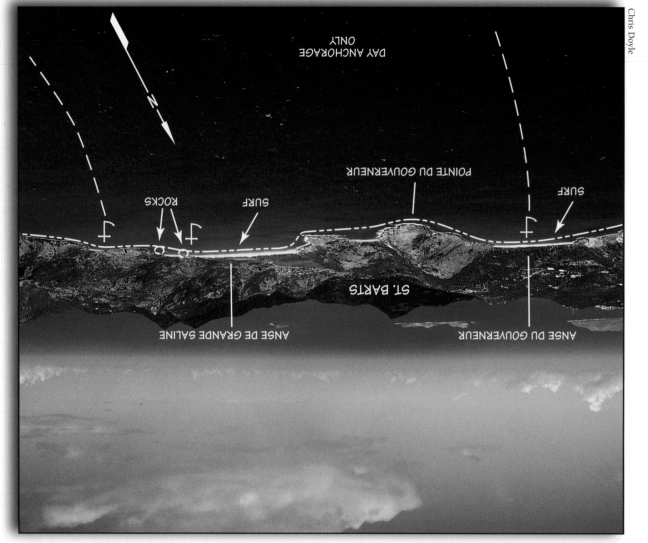

Chris Doyle

DAY ANCHORAGE
ONLY

N

ROCKS

SURF

POINTE DU GOUVERNEUR

SURF

ANSE DE GRANDE SALINE

ST. BARTS

ANSE DU GOUVERNEUR

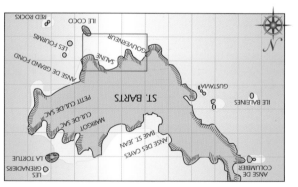

RED ROCKS
ILE COCO
LES FOURMIS
GOUVERNEUR
SALINE
ANSE DE GRAND FOND
ST. BARTS
GUSTAVIA
ILE BALEINES
MARIGOT
CUL-DE-SAC
PETIT CUL-DE-SAC
BAIE ST. JEAN
ANSE DES CAYES
LA TORTUE
LES GRENADIERS
ANSE DE COLUMBIER
N

Anse de Grande Saline and Anse du Gouverneur are two fabulous secluded beaches surrounded by scenic cliffs. They are not really anchorages and are totally untenable in strong winds or in any southeasterly wind. However, on a calm day with a light easterly or northeasterly breeze, it is possible to hang in here for lunch. Do not try to anchor unless it is calm and do not stay overnight as conditions could change. Beaching the dinghy could be hazardous.

Anse de Grande Saline is the larger and more protected of the two. You can anchor off the rocks that lie in the northeastern corner. There is another small hidden bay a little farther toward the headland. Although small, this is perhaps the most protected spot, but take care as the wind can swing around onto the shore.

Anse du Gouverneur is also acceptable as a lunch spot on calm days. Anchor off the western end of the beach. Do not attempt to get too close to shore.

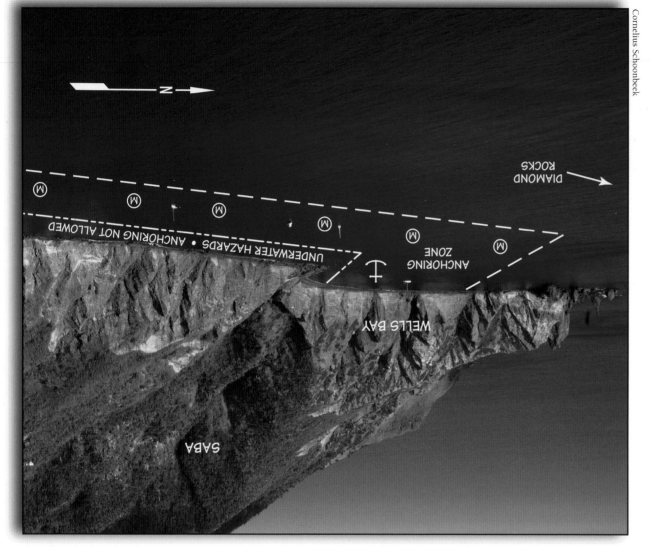

Cornelius Schoonbeek

DIAMOND
ROCKS

WELLS BAY

SABA

UNDERWATER HAZARDS • ANCHORING NOT ALLOWED

ANCHORING
ZONE

N

Saba looks like a fairy tale picture of a forbidden land. A mere 5 square miles, it reaches a lofty 3000 feet. Tall cliffs of red, pink, and brown rise almost vertically from the sea. Houses sit perched in seemingly impossible positions on the edges of precipices. Saba can be untenable in northeasterly winds and swells. Approaching is no problem as the island is steep to and a quarter of a mile will keep you clear of all dangers, except for Diamond Rock and Green Island at the north end.

Most of the time the west coast offers excellent anchorage in either Ladder Bay or Wells Bay. Seven yacht moorings, yellow and blue striped, are spaced on this stretch of coast. They are suitable for yachts up to 60 feet or 50 tons. They are available on a first come basis at no extra charge. You may not anchor close to shore which is all a marine park.

The swell here is comfortably long and gentle, though if the tides are running strongly, you can lie beam to the swells for a few hours on the rising tide. However, this coast is totally open to the north, and should a swell come from this direction, the anchorages will be extremely uncomfortable or even untenable.

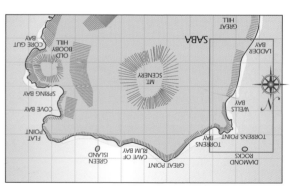

GREAT
HILL

SABA

OLD
BOOBY
HILL

CORE GUT
BAY

SPRING BAY

MT.
SCENERY

COVE BAY

FLAT
POINT

GREEN
ISLAND

GREAT POINT

CAVE OF
RUM BAY

TORRENS
BAY

TORRENS POINT

WELLS
BAY

LADDER
BAY

DIAMOND
ROCKS

N

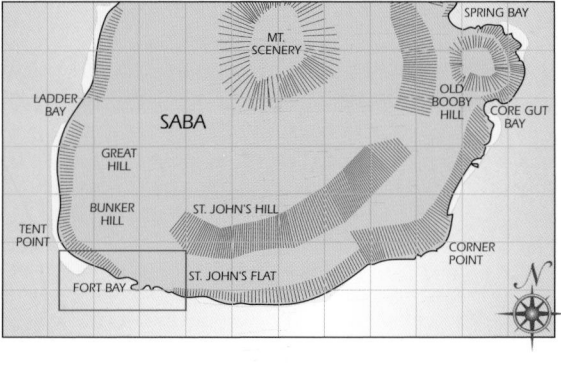

SABA

Harbor Master
Marine Park
Office

To Bottom

LEO CHANCE PIER

ⓂⓂⓂ

NO ANCHORING ZONE
OUTSIDE OF HARBOR AREA

Cornelius Schoonbeek

Fort Bay is the only harbor on Saba. All you will find there is a way to get ashore, the harbor officials, dives shops, a rather noisy generator and one restaurant.

Anchoring off Fort Bay is possible but uncomfortable. You would not want to be here in a southeast wind or large southerly swells. However, this is the only reasonable anchorage in northerly swells or strong northeasterly winds. The bottom shelves quickly, so you have to anchor quite close to shore.

There are a couple of safe moorings available outside the harbor. These can take yachts of any size or even a small cruise ship. Yachts are welcome to use them free of charge when they are available. Call the harbormaster on VHF: 16/11. If you do use a mooring, make sure you are properly secured and let out plenty of scope. If you just want a night in port while you have dinner out, you can talk to the harbormaster about going into the harbor and tying alongside the wall, but you would not normally be able to stay long.

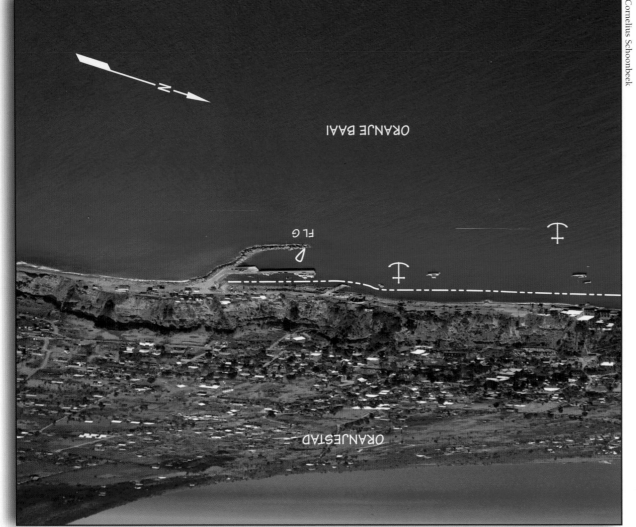

Cornelius Schoonbeek

ORANJE BAAI

FL G

ORANJESTAD

Oranjestad, Statia

Statia is a small peaceful island with the distinctive Quill Volcano dominating the southeastern part. Ashore you will find shops, restaurants and great hiking.

Oranje Baai is the only real anchorage. For most of the time it is perfectly acceptable and calm. However, it is no place to be in a disturbed weather system including a bad northerly swell. Regular easterly swells bend round the island arriving in Oranje Baai from the south. You can get out of these swells by anchoring behind the new breakwater. The Statia Marine Park has put moorings in the most protected area, allowing more yachts to share it. Look for the yellow buoys, both spar and round. Each has a pick up line attached to a smaller buoy. Pick up the loop and put your dock line though the plastic eye at the end, keeping it as short as possible. You may anchor away from these buoys, but the park charges all boats $10.00 US a night, on or off moorings.

The port has a dinghy dock well in on the shore side of the main ship dock. You can also tie your dinghy to the baby dock. A green flashing light marks the end of the dock. There are red lights on the hills to the north of Oranjestad marking the airport.

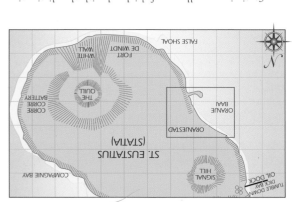

ST. EUSTATIUS (STATIA)

COMPAGNIE BAY
SIGNAL HILL
TUMBLE DOWN DICK BAY
OIL DOCK
ORANJESTAD
ORANJE BAAI
THE QUILL
CORRE CORRE BATTERY
WHITE WALL
FORT DE WINDT
FALSE SHOAL

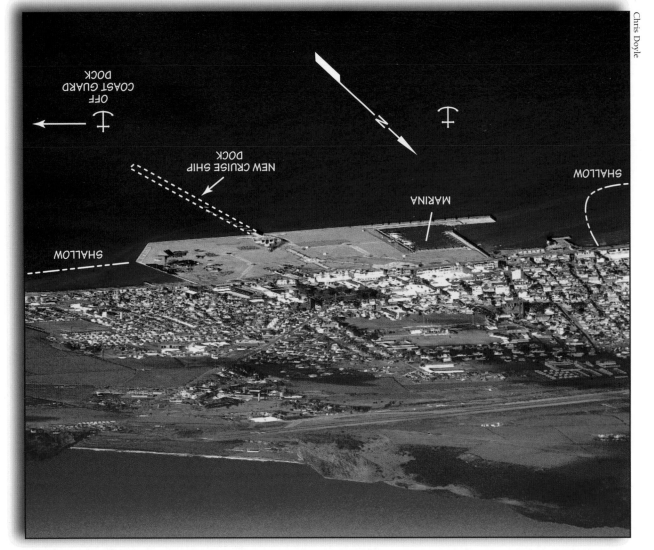

Chris Doyle

Basseterre is the site of the original French settlement in St. Kitts. It is a delightful old town built along the waterfront with architecture that varies from solid British to fancy French. It was largely rebuilt after a fire in 1876.

The large cruise ship dock has been damaged several times in hurricanes and some debris may still remain close to it.

Basseterre is open and faces south. It is well protected in easterly or northeasterly winds, but when wind and swell shifts round to southeast, it becomes very uncomfortable and it is not unusual to have short seas over two feet high rolling in.

The new marina gives the great convenience of being able to walk ashore right in town. However, it is also subject to southerly swells and can be unmanageable in southerly winds.

Modifications are to be made to the marina to make it more protected. You can also anchor about half a mile east of the marina off the deep-water harbor just in front of the coast guard dock. Keep in water at least 14-20 feet deep.

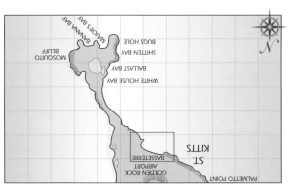

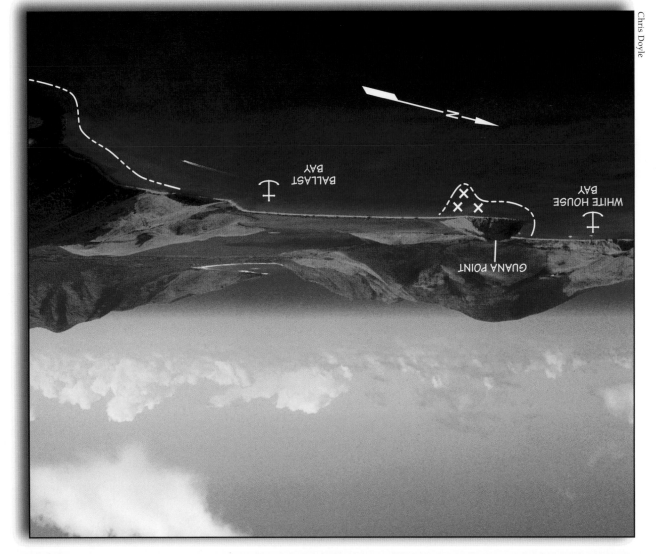

Chris Doyle

BALLAST BAY

WHITE HOUSE BAY

GUANA POINT

N

MOSQUITO BLUFF

BANANA BAY

MAJOR'S BAY

SHITTEN BAY

BUGS HOLE

WHITE HOUSE BAY

BALLAST BAY

ST. KITTS

BASSETERRE

GOLDEN ROCK AIRPORT

PALMETTO POINT

N

White House and Ballast Bays are two well-protected bays, often much calmer than Basseterre. There are no shore facilities, but this is a delightful anchoring area amid beautiful scenery with good snorkeling.

The only navigational hazard, a long reef which sticks out from Guana Point, lies between the two bays. Give it good clearance. White House Bay is much smaller, but nearer the road if you want to tour the island. Anchor off the old dock ruins in the middle of the bay in 19 to 20 feet of water. It is sandy close to shore, rocky farther out. There is a reef to the south of the dock decorated by an interesting old wreck and there are a few underwater rocks that come out a couple of hundred feet from the shore in this area. Ballast Bay is much larger with a long stony beach and lots of century plants. Once you are clear of the reef off Guana Point you can anchor anywhere.

Charlestown/Pinney's Beach, Nevis

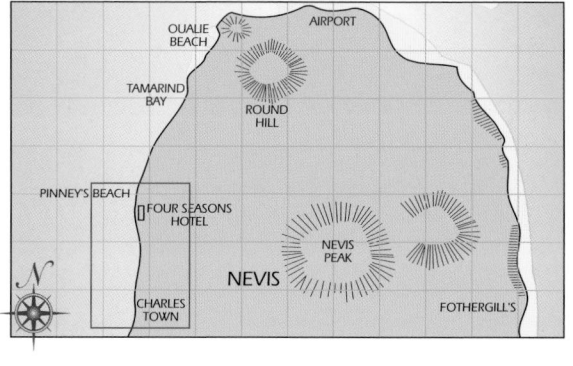

Charlestown, Nevis's only town, is picturesque with many historic buildings of stone and wood. The renovated waterfront area has a pleasant square facing the dinghy dock. Great little shops abound and there are plenty of restaurants.

If approaching from the south, stay a few hundred yards off Fort Charles as it is shallow some way out. Anchor anywhere in the bay, but leave a clear passage for the ferries into the dock.

The bottom off Charlestown is mainly sand, with a few large rocks around. Do not anchor close to shore in case a large swell builds up. The anchorage at the north of town just off Pinney's Beach is fabulous.

Behind a strip of pale ochre sand are miles of palm trees whose slender trunks and waving lacy leaves catch the sunlight. Mt. Nevis ascends into the clouds behind. Gliding pelicans fold their wings and crash boldly in the sea. St. Kitts lying to the north, appears to be part of Nevis in a sweeping panorama. The Four Seasons Hotel on Pinney's Beach makes a conspicuous landmark.

Pinney's Beach goes on for nearly three miles and you can anchor just about anywhere. The further north you go the more secluded it gets.

Chris Doyle

Chris Doyle

Tamarind Bay

This fine small anchorage is three miles north of Charlestown and is one of the calmest in Nevis. It is just beyond Pinney's Beach but still within sight of it. It has its own small sand beach, which occasionally turns to stone after heavy swells.

If coming from Charlestown, follow Pinney's Beach, then continue over toward Cades Point. Turn into Tamarind Bay and anchor in nine to twelve feet of water. The holding is good in sand, when you get through the weed. A few rocks, colonized by resting pelicans, mark the south end of the beach.

Oualie Beach

Oualie Beach is in a pleasant bay, but is somewhat shoal. A shelf of sand and weed with depths of only 4 to 6 feet extends several hundred yards out from the middle of the bay. This breaks in heavy swells. However, if you make a sweep well outside the bay and come in close to Hurricane Hill, there is about 9 feet of water close to the hill. There is plenty of room for one or two deep draft yachts as well as several shoal draft boats to anchor. You can use the dinghy dock at the Oualie Beach Hotel, but make sure you tie up clear of the end part used by the dive and fishing boats.

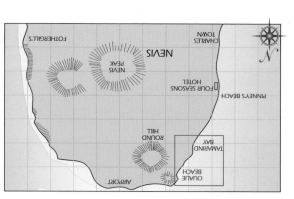

BARBUDA

SPANISH POINT

N

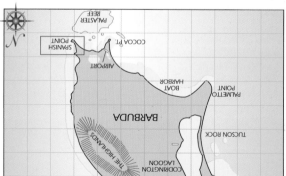

This is a quiet anchorage tucked among the reefs in brilliant turquoise water. Ashore there is a small beach. You can just see the ruin of an old fort to the north. The nearest habitation is Coco Point Lodge.

The approach is inside the reef that extends southwest from Spanish Point. Inshore there are isolated patches of brown reef. Anchor outside these in 10 feet of water, about 150 yards off the beach. This anchorage is especially easy if you enter by the eastern route. You come through the channel, and then follow the reef around into the anchorage.

There are some marvelous walks here especially up the windward coast which has endless spectacular beaches. If you see wild donkeys, do not approach too closely as the males are quite protective. A rough road leads to Cocoa Point. Wherever you anchor, you will be within easy swimming distance of at least one reef. Snorkeling on the small isolated reefs is excellent for beginners; the reef off Spanish Point will satisfy the enthusiast.

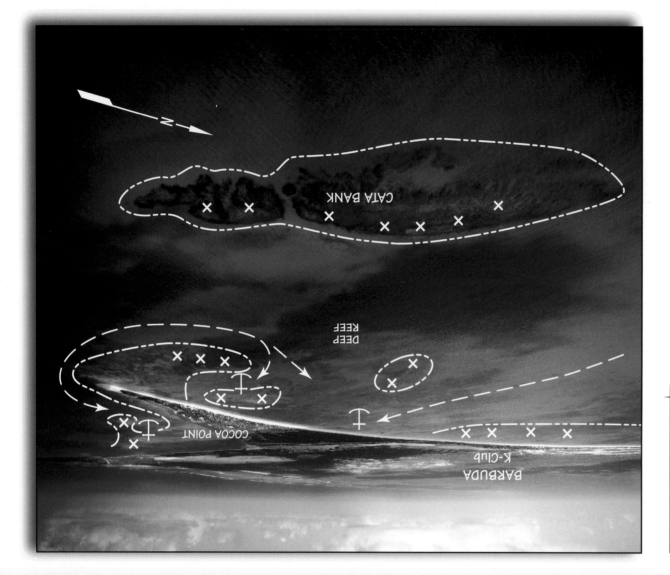

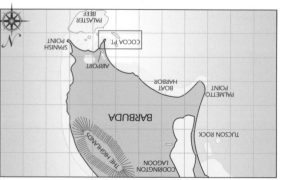

The anchorage to the west of Cocoa Point is a favorite due to the miles of pristine creamy-pink beach. If you are approaching from the south coast, head over to Cocoa Point and follow the reef closely. Once you are clear of the reef, head in toward the beach between the two hotels. There is a line of buoys in front of the Cocoa Point Lodge reserving the area for their own water sports. When they are closed (May – October) this is not a problem. Be careful of the extensive reefs that start at the north end of this anchorage and continue way past the K- Club.

To the east of Cocoa Point there is a small basin of water, 11 feet deep, just opposite the dock on the back side of Cocoa Point Lodge. The entrance is a narrow cut between two reefs. It is best to identify the reef adjoining Cocoa Point and follow it down to the opening. Once inside you have reef protection from all around.

Chris Doyle

FALMOUTH
HARBOUR

ANTIGUA

PROCTORS
POINT

NO ANCHORING   BUOYED CHANNEL

DIEPPE
BAY

BISHOP SHOAL

ANTIGUA YACHT
CLUB MARINA

ENGLISH HARBOUR

FALMOUTH HARBOUR
MARINA

CATAMARAN
CLUB MARINA

ANTIGUA

WILLOUGHBY BAY

YORK
ISLAND

GREEN
ISLAND

INDIAN CREEK

MAMORA BAY

ENGLISH
HARBOUR

FALMOUTH
HARBOUR

CARLISLE BAY

Falmouth Harbour, Antigua

Falmouth Harbour is large well-protected bay with lots of anchoring room as well as many major marinas. It is a major yachting center and the winter home of many gold-plated charter yachts of sail and power. There is usually a good breeze here making for a pleasant, cool anchorage.

Entering Falmouth Harbour presents no special problems. Keep well clear of Bishop Shoal and then either head up toward the yacht club, staying inside the red buoy that marks the middle reef, or line up the two bright orange triangular day markers and head over to the Catamaran Hotel and Marina. Do not anchor in the exclusion zone in front of The Yacht Club Marina and Falmouth Harbour Marina. Falmouth Harbour Marina has had problems with yachts anchoring too close. If you keep west of the closest of John Bentley's mooring buoys, you will be okay. Large yachts using the marinas sometimes end up with entwined anchors.

Ashore there are several large marinas, plenty of restaurants and shops, as well as services and chandleries for yachts.

Chris Doyle

SHIRLEY HEIGHTS

CHARLOTTE POINT

FREEMAN BAY

KEEP CLEAR

FORT BERKELY PT.

ANTIGUA SLIPWAY

NELSON'S DOCKYARD

TANK BAY

CUSTOMS

ORDNANCE BAY

ANTIGUA

ENGLISH HARBOUR

N

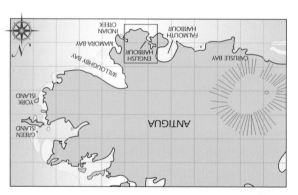

ANTIGUA

GREEN ISLAND

YORK ISLAND

WILLOUGHBY BAY

MAMORA BAY

ENGLISH HARBOUR

FALMOUTH HARBOUR

INDIAN CREEK

CARLISLE BAY

N

English Harbour is a secure harbor protected enough to ride out a hurricane. It was a major British naval base from 1723 when work was begun on the English Harbour Dockyard. It was completed as it stands today in around 1745 and was Britain's main naval station in the Lesser Antilles. Nelson was stationed here in 1784 under Sir Richard Hughes and eventually took over as naval commander. The dockyard is now generally known as Nelson's Dockyard. When former commander Vernon Nicholson sailed into English Harbour in 1947, the dockyard was in ruins. The arrival of Nicholson's Charter Company and the restoration of the ruins into a beautiful yet functional monument gave momentum to the development of the yachting industry here. Today English Harbour and Falmouth Harbours are both the yachting capital of Antigua, and a major Caribbean yachting center.

Entering English Harbour presents no special problems. Avoid the rock shoal off Charlotte Point. Do not anchor in the channel marked. You can anchor in Freeman Bay, or way up in the harbor, or stern to the Dockyard or Antigua Slipway.

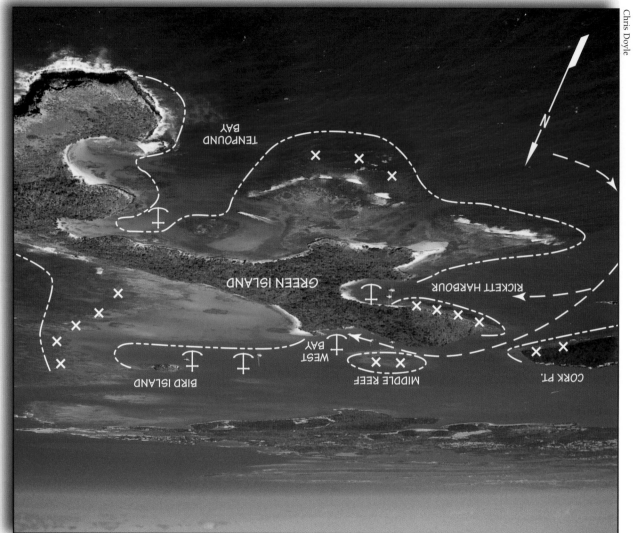

Chris Doyle

TENPOUND BAY

GREEN ISLAND

RICKETT HARBOUR

CORK PT.

WEST BAY

MIDDLE REEF

BIRD ISLAND

N

ANTIGUA

YORK ISLAND

WILLOUGHBY BAY

MAMORA BAY

ENGLISH HARBOUR

FALMOUTH HARBOUR

INDIAN CREEK

CARLISLE BAY

GREEN ISLAND

N

Green Island is Antigua's eastern most point. It is the gateway to Nonsuch Bay, a reef-protected expanse of water covering several square miles. This offers a wealth of good overnight anchorages. The north side of Green Island is protected by a barrier reef. You can find comfortable anchorage inside the reef anywhere between Green Island and Bird Island, in a vast expanse of turquoise water.

Enter halfway between Green Island and Cork Point, then stay fairly close to Green Island to avoid the big Middle Reef. The water immediately north of Green Island tends to be shallow, but it gets deeper toward Bird Island. You can see this in the color of the water. Tenpound Bay is charming but the anchorage is so tiny that two boats are a crowd and there is barely room to turn round inside. Drop your mainsail before you enter, as there may not be enough room to come head to the wind in the channel. The anchorage may be rolly in southeasterly winds.

Rickett Harbour is lovely. Watch for the large reef that extends southwards between Tenpound Bay and Rickett Harbour. Follow it round into the bay. You will find good anchorage with plenty of room in 10 to 18 feet of water with a sand bottom.

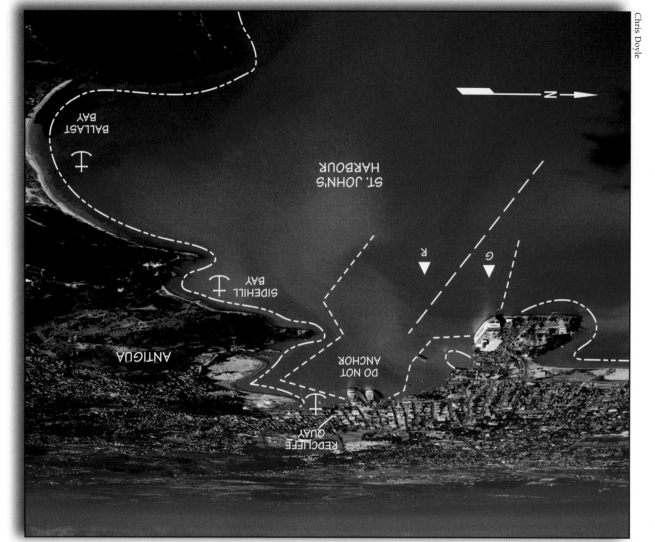

Chris Doyle

BALLAST BAY

ST. JOHN'S HARBOUR

SIDEHILL BAY

ANTIGUA

R

G

DO NOT ANCHOR

REDCLIFFE QUAY

N

ANTIGUA

GUANA ISLAND

GREAT BIRD ISLAND

MAIDEN IS.

LONG ISLAND

ST JOHN'S

DICKENSON BAY

PRICKLY PEAR ISLAND

DEEP BAY

FIVE ISLAND HARBOUR

N

St. John's is the capital of Antigua. It is an attractive city, with carefully restored old buildings as well as rough old buildings full of local color. The convenience of major supermarkets, good restaurants, and a local produce market, along with countless boutiques, and handicraft shops, which have been developed with cruise ship passengers in mind, all have their appeal. The main channel is dredged from 28 to 35 feet deep. It includes a large maneuvering area in front of Heritage Quay. It is buoyed according to IALA B (red right returning). Under no circumstances should you anchor in the channel. Anchor on either side of the main channel. The best spot is in town off Redcliffe Quay where you will find 10 to 12 feet - but it is subject to shoaling. Redcliffe Quay has some docks where you can come stern-to.

Deep Bay, Antigua

Chris Doyle

Deep Bay is a charming anchorage with a long sandy beach. It is the home of the mammoth Royal Antiguan, which is end on to the bay and does not affect the view.

The wreck of the Andes is right in the middle of the bay. A few mast stumps stick about two feet above water. You can pass on either side, but a broken mast lies south of the wreck, so do not pass too close. Anchor off the beach in about 10 to 12 feet of water. Although this anchorage is normally well protected, it can roll in northerly swells.

Snorkeling or diving on the wreck of the Andes is great. This three masted iron barque was sailing from Trinidad to Peru with a load of pitch in 1905. When it got to Antigua the crew noticed smoke rising from the hollow masts indicating a fire. Being a hazardous cargo, they were refused permission to go into St. Johns, so they anchored in Deep Bay. When they opened the cargo hatches to deal with the fire the infusion of fresh air caused the pitch to burst into flame. The wreck sits upright on the bottom encrusted with sponges and coral.

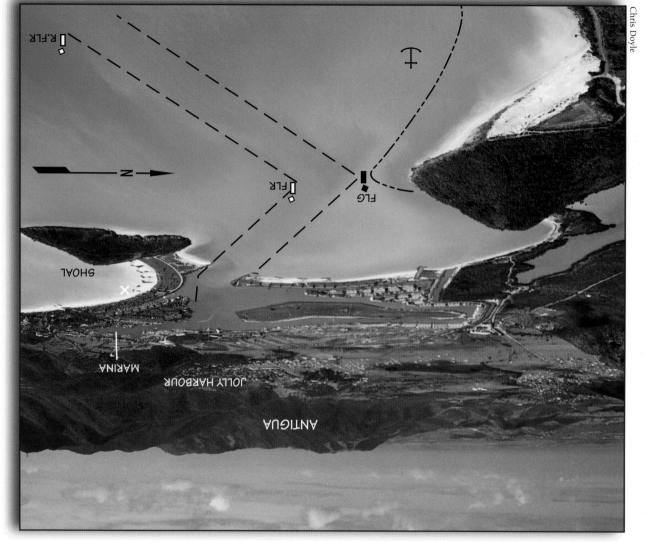

Chris Doyle

Jolly Harbour is a large, new, full service marina and condominium development, with over seven miles of dredged waterfront. It is very well protected. It is also a port of entry with the customs and immigration station near the fuel dock.

The marina channel was dredged to 17 feet. Current information indicates there is still 13 feet all the way in, with a very soft bottom. Boats much over 11 feet should call the marina for the latest depth information. Deep draft yachts should come from the west, approaching Five Islands at about 105° magnetic and then plotting a course to take them north of Irish Bank before they approach the dredged channel. The dredged channel is marked by beacons and buoys (red, right, returning). The outer red beacon and both sides of the channel turning mark are lit by flashing lights. There is always plenty of room in the marina as well as moorings.

Those seeking anchorage outside the marina can feel their way out of the channel before the turning marks. The most pleasant anchorage is to the north of the channel, off the beach. While most of this area is currently 7 to 12 feet deep, approach cautiously as depths have been known to change.

Deshaies, Guadeloupe

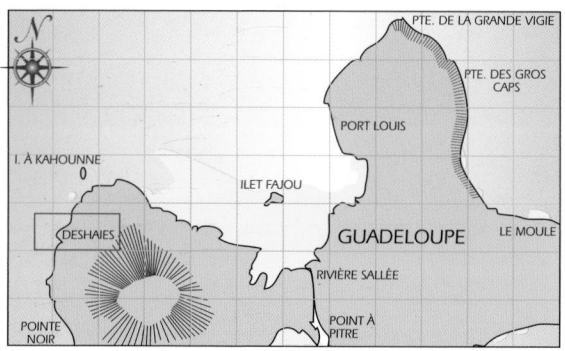

Deshaies (pronounced Day-hay) is a deep, well-protected bay, surrounded by hills and mountains. A breakwater forms a harbor for small fishing boats close to the entrance to the river. Attractions include a tropical river and the picturesque village of Deshaies, built right on the beach. A breakwater forms a harbor for small fishing boats close to the entrance to the river.

Enter the middle of the bay and anchor anywhere inside. Sometimes the wind comes regularly from the town, other times it is light and variable.

There is a customs office in Deshaies that does not have regular hours, however they leave forms for you can fill out and post in a box beside the office. If you are visiting other ports in Guadeloupe, or you need clearance for your next port, make sure you catch them to get the proper paperwork.

Chris Doyle

Chris Doyle

GUADELOUPE

COUSTEAU NATIONAL PARK

PIGEON ISLAND

N

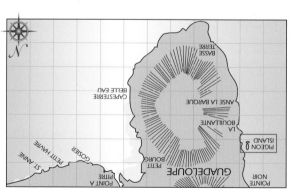

GUADELOUPE

POINTE NOIR

PIGEON ISLAND

PETIT BOURG

POINT A PITRE

PETIT HAVRE

ST. ANNE

GOSIER

LA BOUILLANTE

ANSE LA BARQUE

CAPESTERRE BELLE EAU

BASSE TERRE

N

The main attraction here is the Cousteau Under-water Park, which includes the islands and the coast northwards for about a mile. This is an excellent place for scuba diving. Fishing is strictly forbidden. There are red and white mooring buoys dotted around the island. The white ones sometimes go adrift and the authorities only replace them occasion-ally. The white buoys are for yachts and the red ones for the professional groups. We noticed dinghies tied to the red ones. If you do this, try to raft alongside other dinghies and keep out of the way of the dive boats. Anchoring in the park is not allowed.

You may find it calmer to anchor overnight in the bay opposite Pigeon Island. The rocky shore is bro-ken by two sandy beaches. The smaller one is more secluded, the larger one more popular, with several shacks selling snacks, along with dive shops. Enter the bay in the center and anchor in 12 to 16 feet of water. Holding is variable so make sure that you are well dug in. The wind can swing around so those on rope are advised to use two anchors. A stern anchor can help cut down roll if there is any swell. The view of the islands from the anchorage makes a perfect sunset photo.

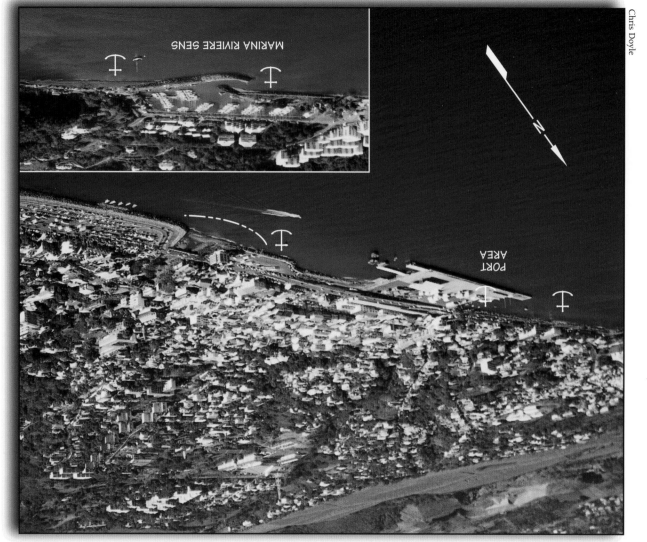

Chris Doyle

MARINA RIVIERE SENS

PORT AREA

N

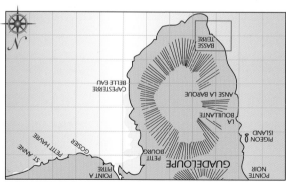

Basse Terre is the capital of Guadeloupe. The architecture is a blend of old and new, brick and wood with handsome arches. There are many small shops, boutiques, and a good fresh food market.

The approach to Basse Terre is deep. The best place for yachts is at the Marina Rivière Sens about a mile south of town. Maximum depth is 7 feet, with shallower rocks, enter cautiously. If there is space, you can enter and tie up to the visitors dock. There are red buoys for each space, you tie onto the red buoy and go bow or stern to the dock.

Take care when entering as recent storms placed some large boulders in the channel between the breakwaters.

The best anchorage is off the marina entrance on a shelf, which varies from 15 to 45 feet with good holding. You can also anchor south of the marina off the black sand beach in 30 feet of water.

It is also permitted to anchor off town, at either end of the large ship dock in about 25 feet of water. There are low wharves where you can leave your dinghy. The anchorage to the north of the dock is normally calmer than the one to the south. However it does roll and the marina is a better option.

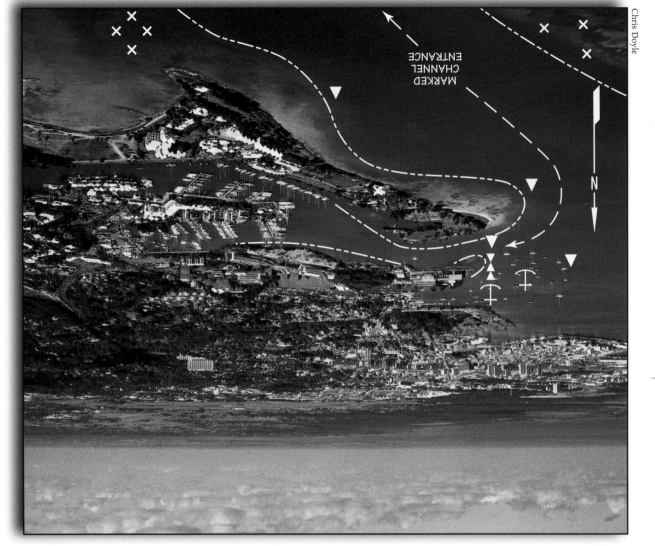

Chris Doyle

MARKED CHANNEL ENTRANCE

N

Pointe à Pitre, Guadeloupe's largest and most important city, is a lively Créole town with a hodge-podge of old and new buildings. It is well protected in a waterway between Grand Terre and Basse Terre. Port du Plaisance, more properly known as Port de Plaisance de Bas du Fort, is inside the harbor entrance, about a 20-minute walk to town. This whole area is geared to yachts, and this is one of the best yachting service centers in the Leewards. The channel is well marked by buoys. Yachts either go into the marina or anchor outside, or along the coast towards the city. Anchoring is not allowed in the main channel.

When entering the marina, leave the red buoys to starboard. Leave both the yellow and black one and all the green ones to port.

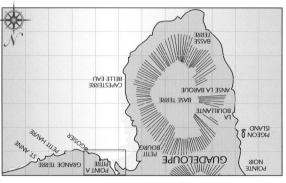

N

GUADELOUPE

BASSE TERRE
BASE TERRE
CAPESTERRE BELLE EAU
ANSE LA BARQUE
LA BOUILLANTE
PIGEON ISLAND
POINTE NOIR
PETIT HAVRE
GOSIER
ST. ANNE
GRANDE TERRE
POINT A PITRE
PETIT BOURG

Ilet à Gosier, Guadeloupe

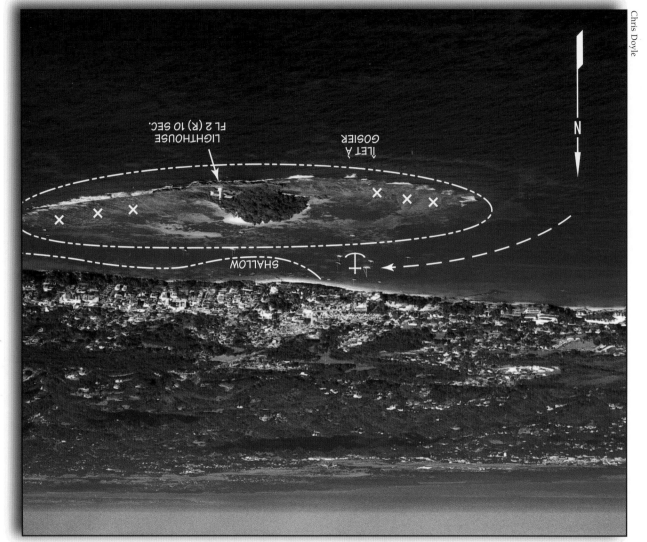

Chris Doyle

N

LIGHTHOUSE
FL 2 (R) 10 SEC.

ÎLET A GOSIER

SHALLOW

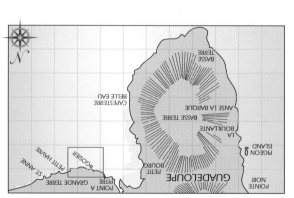

N

GUADELOUPE

POINTE NOIR

PIGEON ISLAND

LA BOUILLANTE

BASSE TERRE

BASSE TERRE

CAPESTERRE BELLE EAU

ANSE LA BAROUE

PETIT BOURG

GRANDE TERRE

POINT A PITRE

ST. ANNE

PETIT HAVRE

GOSIER

Ilet à Gosier is a tiny wooded island, partially surrounded by reefs, with soft white sand beaches, and a pleasantly old fashioned lighthouse. It is only three miles from Pointe à Pitre.

From Pointe à Pitre it is simple to follow the coast down to Ilet à Gosier. Sailing from the Saintes, you can see the town of Gosier, with smallish cliffs on either side. The feature that stands out most in sunlight, is a contemporary church spire that is oblong and looks like an apartment building that has been through a French fry machine. As you get closer, the lighthouse becomes visible. Approach the anchorage from the Pointe à Pitre side and eyeball your way in slowly. Once you are inside the reef, the sea bed shelves gradually up to the island. You can anchor anywhere between Ilet à Gosier and the small town of Gosier in good holding clay-like sand. In theory you can carry seven feet through the pass between the island and the mainland. In practice, it is not worth trying . The bottom is a patchwork of sand and weed and it is hard to tell the shallow spots from the deeper spots.

St. François, Guadeloupe

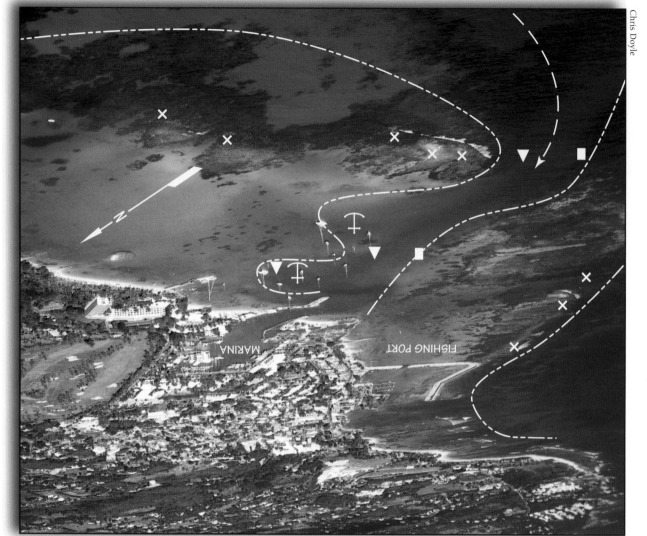

Chris Doyle

MARINA

FISHING PORT

The well-protected reef anchorage at St. François lies between the town and some large hotels. Although the deep water anchorage in this area is quite small, the reef encloses miles of turquoise water, giving a wonderful feeling of space. Add the municipal marina and you get an area that is attractive to yachts-people, yet just too far off the beaten track to be crowded by yachts.

St. François has two harbors: a fishing port in front of the town, which is only for small fishing boats, and a large yacht harbor to the east. The outside part of the yacht harbor can take yachts of up to seven and a half foot draft. The entrance is tricky. Enter in good light when you can see the reefs. The channel is narrow and can be very rough. Both wind and sea push you in, so you want to do it right. The harbor entrance is marked by green and red buoys (red, right, returning). Seas often break right up to the first buoys. Do not cut them under any circumstances. It is easiest to approach the entrance a bit from the east. Before you enter make sure you can see the next set of buoys. Once you pass these, the water is relatively calm. You can anchor just north of the channel behind the reef in 8 – 10 feet.

Chris Doyle

PTE DE FOLIE ANSE

St. Louis is the main yacht anchorage in Marie Galante. It is a small rural town surrounded by peaceful countryside with fields of sugar cane and spectacular beaches. Ashore you can buy essentials and find a few restaurants.

The most pleasant anchorage is to the south of the large ferry dock off the beach, you can also anchor north of the ferry dock off town. Do not anchor between the yellow buoy and the fuel tanks ashore, as there are underwater pipes. Depth in the bay is mainly eight to eleven feet, shelving as you approach within a hundred yards of the shore. It is not always easy to distinguish the shallower spots, so approach the beach with caution. The swell in this bay often rocks you gently. In a northeaster it can throw you out of bed. In these conditions you would find it better at Grand Bourg.

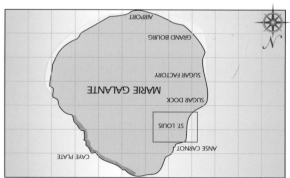

Chris Doyle

Grand Bourg is the main town in Marie Galante. It is a typical country town with a church, several pharmacies and banks, card phones, and some fair supermarkets and restaurants.

A large protective wall has been built, creating a harbor. It is small, not much over 400 feet long and about the same in width. Approach from offshore and enter between the two buoys. Aim for the ferry dock before turning up into the harbor. You can anchor inside. Anchor well clear of the two ferry stations on the ferry dock. Watch the depths as you go in, as the 9 foot basin shelves rapidly toward the shore. There is room for about half a dozen keel boats to swing at anchor and, if they arrive before you, you can drop a stern anchor and run a bow line onto the east wall. Take an anchor to wedge in, or tie your line around a large rock. The bottom of the harbor is hard coral covered with a layer of mud that gets thinner as you go towards shore. You can also anchor outside, just to the west of the harbor, but this is much less protected and liable to roll especially when the ferries arrive.

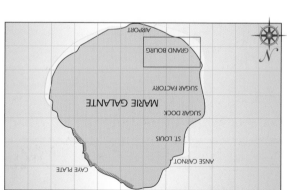

The Saintes are an irresistible group of islands, with an idyllic Gallic charm. The only small town, Bourg des Saintes, is on the largest island, Terre D'en Haut. The Saintes have been French since shortly after they were colonized, and have long supported a small community, which used to rely almost entirely on fishing. There is a strong link to the north of France, especially Brittany.

From the north it is easiest to enter between Le Pate and Ilet à Cabrit. Besides several shoals along the coast, there are a couple of obvious dangers to watch out for. One is the coral patch between Ilet à Cabrit and Tête Rouge (on Terre d'en Haut). It is normally marked by an unlit red and black buoy just to its southeast. This was missing in 2001. The shoal is visible is good light and you can pass on either side. The passage is wider between the shoal and Tête Rouge.

Anchor anywhere off the town, but leave a wide berth for the ferries. The sand close to the main ferry dock is hard and may prove difficult for some anchors. It is sometimes rolly by the fishing harbor, but holding is better. You can also find good anchorage in Ilet à Cabrit and on the west side of Pain de Sucre.

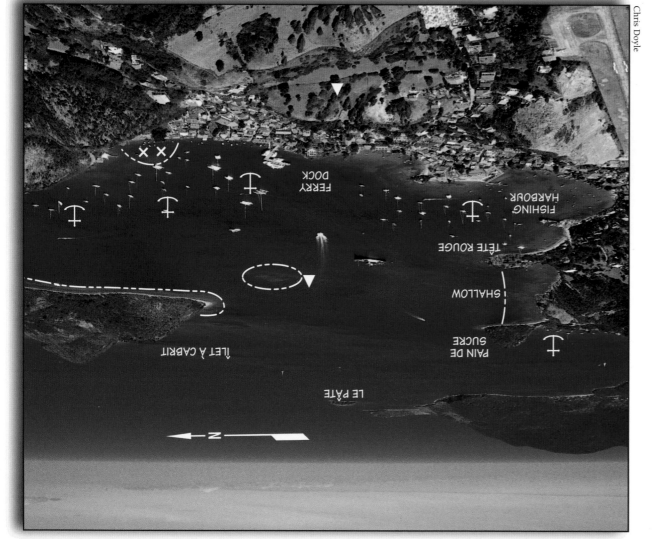

Chris Doyle

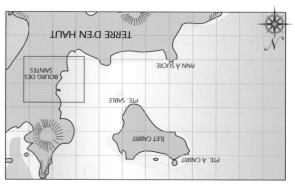

Chris Doyle

COCONUT BEACH

PURPLE TURTLE

SUNSHINE VILLAGE

THE CABRITS

ROLLO HEAD

N

This protected bay is over two miles long and a mile wide. It is set in magnificent scenery with the small town of Portsmouth at its head. Under normal conditions you can anchor almost anywhere off the coast from the Coconut Beach Hotel on the south shore right around to Sunshine Village on the north. Most yachts anchor off the beach a little to the north of Portsmouth in the area of the Purple Turtle. This is the calmest spot in northerly swells. In this area you should anchor in less than 40 feet of water, as there are coral heads in the deeper water. Coral growths can also be found between the cruise ship dock and the Purple Turtle close to shore. If you want to anchor in the shallower water, snorkel and take a look. Holding is good in sand if you avoid the coral heads. From the anchorage it is easy to get to town or to the Cabrits National Park.

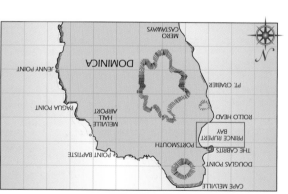

N

DOMINICA

MERO CASTAWAYS

JENNY POINT

PT. CRABIER

PAGUA POINT

MELVILLE HALL AIRPORT

ROLLO HEAD

PRINCE RUPERT BAY

PORTSMOUTH

POINT BAPTISTE

THE CABRITS

DOUGLAS POINT

CAPE MELVILLE

Prince Rupert Bay, Dominica

Roseau, Dominica

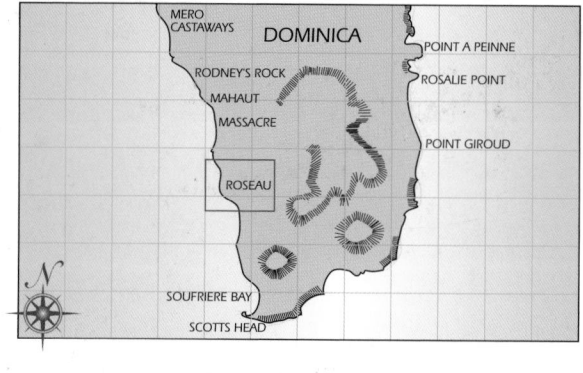

Roseau is the capital of Dominica. Of all the islands, this city has the most wonderful assortment of authentic and lovely Caribbean buildings. The most convenient anchorage is in the area of the Anchorage Hotel, a mile south of town. The Anchorage Hotel is modern and white and has a largish dock. There is a fairly wide shelf on which to anchor. It is best to go bow or stern to the shore, tying up to the hotel wall or to the trees northwards of the Anchorage. Avoid anchoring close to the docks and mooring buoys used by dive boats. Do not tie too close to the beach or you may find yourself on the surf-line in case of a large swell. Large yachts, should anchor near the Fort Young Hotel which has a great new landing dock.

Chris Doyle